This workbook is for your personal use—if you have purchased a digital copy, please feel free to print a copy for yourself. Other than your personal copy, physical or digital, no part of this publication may be stored, reproduced, or transmitted in any form or by any means, electronic, mechanical, photocopying, recording, scanning, or otherwise, except as permitted under Section 107 or 108 of the 1976 United States Copyright Act, without the prior written permission of the author. Permission requests to the author and publisher may be emailed to: info@annodright.com.

Limitation of liability/disclaimer of warranty: While the publisher and author have used their best efforts in preparing this work, they make no representations or warranties with respect to the accuracy or completeness of the contents of this document and specifically disclaim any implied warranties of merchantability or appropriateness for particular purpose. No warranty may be created or extended by sales representatives, promoters, colleagues, or written sales materials.

The advice and strategies contained herein may 'not be suitable for your situation. You should consult with a professional where appropriate. Neither the publisher nor author shall be liable for any damages or results.

This workbook is designed to provide accurate and authoritative information in regard to the subject matter covered. This workbook is sold with the understanding that the publisher is not engaged in rendering psychological, financial, legal, or other professional services. If expert assistance or counseling is needed, the services of a competent professional should be sought.

It Takes A Village. Here is mine:

Workbook Designed by Dalychia Saah
Cover Illustration by Esther Luntadila
Feelings Chart by Donald Harris Jr.
Other Illustrations by Rochelle Johnson

ISBN: 13:978-1-7337549-0-3

Copyright © 2019 ANNODRIGHT, LLC
All rights reserved. This book or any portion thereof may not be reproduced or used in any manner whatsoever without the express written permission of the publisher except for the use of brief quotations in a book review.

Dedication:

"Her Skin Absorbs The Sun's Rays, Her Hair Defies Gravity. You Can't Tell Me Black Women Aren't Magical". ~Unknown

This workbook is dedicated to Black women who continue to be seen as less than in a world which favors whiteness. You are already all that and a bag of chips!

Acknowledgements

Birthing this workbook was not the work of one person alone. It took a village. My village included my coach and friend, Dr. Ajita Robinson of the Private Practice Academy, who wouldn't take my excuses and expected more from me. Dr. Joy Harden Bradford of Therapy For Black Girls, who made sure I had some follow through and told the folk before I was done. To my partner, Brian, who always knew I would do things anyway and was just waiting on me to know. And to my family (Papa, Gracie, Bose, Felicia, and Krys-mas) who always supports me in everything. No matter what.

I also want to thank the wonderful team of folk who helped put this bad boy together. From editing, to artistry, and beyond. Dalychia of AFROSEXOLOGY, got design chops! Thank you for keeping me on task and checking in with me. Thanks for your suggestions, and for your passion for this work. Donald of DesignedByDonald, thank you for taking all the time needed to create the feelings chart. You knew what it meant to me to get that right in a world that would rather make things neutral by making them yellow, you gave us Black women, in all their emotional glory! To Esther, of 4everetherr (on Instagram) the artist of the cover design, who plucked what I didn't know I wanted right out of my head and made it a reality! To Roe of RoeDesignes (on Instagram), creator of coloring pages and descriptive art, I am so glad I found a Morgan State Alum to work on this project! We are the Bears, all day, everyday! And to my never failing assistant Kia! Stepping up into all this work and owning it like only you do! Thank you!

Table of Contents

Welcome..7

How Do I use this workbook?...8

Terms To Know..10

Getting To The Basics: It's A Goal Thing..13

Pre-work WERK..16

Feelings Chart...23

Journal Prompts..24

- Month 1 (weeks 1-4)..26
- Month 2 (weeks 5-8)..40
   - Story Time...49
- Month 3 (weeks 9-12)..63
   - Challenge Day: 14 Days of Praise..72
   - Not Another Story...80

Activities..83

It's Coloring Time..95

Challenges..103

You Did It!..116

My Thoughts...121

Answer Key...126

Resources...130

Meet The Author..133

References..134

"YOU CANNOT STOP BIRDS FROM FLYING OVER YOUR HEAD, BUT YOU CAN STOP THEM FROM NESTING IN YOUR HAIR."
—African Proverb

This workbook belongs to

_____

Welcome...

Hey Sunshine,

First, I want to say I see you. I see you doing all that you do in all the ways that you do it, being the super person that you are— working hard, kicking ass, and taking names! But now it's time to work hard, kick ass, and take names for YOU, the same way you do for everyone else when you are at work, with your partner, with your friends, and when you're with your family. But I see you! I see that you picked up this workbook to work on you. And when it comes right down to it, Black women don't often put themselves first, and today you have. That's why I say, I SEE YOU.

Just so we're clear, this is a mash up of a journal and a workbook. It is meant to have space for you to write your thoughts and feelings, as well as to work on some things, mostly related to colorism and texturism. This book was created with women in mind, especially Black women, who have struggled with loving everything there is to love about themselves because the world tells them not to. Women who have received, and maybe given, disparaging comments about hair texture, length, and style or skin tones too dark or too light. This is for you, and those who want to love themselves from the very crowns of their head to the soles of their feet.

The purpose of this workbook is to help you to discover the origins of your hurts and narratives around your hair texture and skin tone. The purpose is to ease that rift and get you to a place where loving all the parts of you becomes all too easy. The goal is to guide you through your story to understand the significance of race, sex, culture, and intersectionality in your life, and help you crawl, walk, run, and dance along your journey to self-realization. The purpose is for you to discover you in a whole new way.

With love,

Dr. Donna Oriowo (Oreo-whoa)

How do I use this Workbook?

This workbook is set up with prompts and questions for reflection, and with activities and challenges for relaxation and continued work. So basically, it can be a lot, and I am cautioning you now to **take your time**! Go through the workbook one page at a time. This isn't meant to be finished in a day. For years we have been told how and who to be. We have been told what makes us valuable or worthless to others. We have been taught all manner of insidious ways to like and love ourselves just a little less than we deserve. It will take time to separate out the things that don't belong to you, rebuild who you are without those messages, and make your own. So no, it can't be done in a day.

This workbook has three months' worth of weekly journal prompts, activities, and challenges. Try not to do them all at once. Best part is, you own this now. So, when you're done and have made it through, you can always live a little, reflect a little more, and begin again. The journey won't be the same, because you won't be the same. As I am always telling my clients, there are levels to this. You may love yourself on level 1 today, but when you're done and do it again, you can be loving yourself on level 10!

Pro Tips:
- Try to pick one consistent time a week to come to this book and answer a prompt, do an activity, and/or just stare in reflection. It makes it feel less overwhelming. And gives you more time to process.

- If you have the physical book, write in pencil or in a colored gel pen. Why? That way when you revisit your answers and go back through, you can write your new answers in a different color than your old ones and see how your answers have evolved, changed, or stayed the same.

- If you have the digital book, there are several ways for you to use this too!

    - You can download this to your iPad or tablet and with your handy pencil write right in the book! HA! And I know you can change your answer colors too!

    - You can keep it on your computer and type your answers into the text boxes using the edit button.

    - You can write the questions and your answers in a journal or a separate document on your computer.

    - And, of course, you can print as you go...if you're ballin' like that with ink and paper.

Just a Quick Note on What this workbook is NOT:

This book is NOT a replacement for therapy with a mental health professional. While I may be one, as the author, I am not *your* therapist. So, no, this book cannot replace the therapeutic relationship with a licensed and trained professional.

This book is also NOT a guarantee to loving all the pieces of yourself. That can take lots of time and assistance. So while I hope that you get a whole new understanding of yourself and learn to love you on a different level, there are NO guarantees that it will happen by the time you reach the end. My suggestion is that a therapist would be of the most help.

Terms to Know

Here are a few terms that may come up in the workbook. This will help you know what I mean by these words.

- Anxiety: fearful anticipation, worry, restlessness, on edge, or irritably about an event or some other outcome (like what folk will think about your new hairstyle)

- Automatic Coping Skill: what is done automatically/without real thought as a way to cope/emotionally soothe self when there is an emotional upheaval.

- Bad Hair: Typically refers to hair that is phenotypically closer to African ancestry, very kinky or coily, dense.[2]

- Colorism: The hierarchical system where lighter skin in privileged over darker skin[3,5]

- Coping Skill: what you do consciously or subconsciously when there is an emotional upheaval. This can be anything from taking a break to counting backward from 100.

- Depression: impacts how you think, feel, and act, loss of interest, may feel sad, empty, hopeless, fatigued or loss of energy

- Explicit: stated outright with no room for confusion

- Good Hair: Hair that is said to be straighter, looser, easier to manage, softer, and/or silkier. Reflective if European ancestry[1,2]

- Hair texture politics: this refers to how hair texture can hinder a person on their life's journey. An example would be not being able to get certain jobs or promotions based on hair texture. It can be how others feel about your hair that can impact your mobility. Another example would be how folk feel that natural hair is not professional.

- Identity: who you are, how you think and feel about yourself, including your personality, beliefs and goals[4]

- Implicit: indirectly stated, not outright, leaves some room for confusion

- Intersectionality: coined by Kimberle Crenshaw, is how race, class and gender meet and intersect to impact how a person or group of folk experience the world in a way that is different and discriminatory than others based on those social constructs.[6]

- Natural Hair: hair that has not had the texture chemically altered by perms, relaxers, texturizers, etc.[1]

- Texture Envy: a combination of being jealous, desire-filled, and wanting a hair texture that someone else has, often because it is seen as more beautiful or favorable.

- Texturism: the hierarchical system where straighter hair is privileged over curlier/coilier/kinkier hair textures[5]

- Trigger: something in your surroundings that sets off an emotion, memory, and/or flashback to another point in time. Often related back to a trauma that was experienced

- Values: the level of importance something holds as it relates to an individual or a group of people. It can dictate how a person navigates certain situations or relationships[4]

"DO NOT LET WHAT YOU CANNOT DO TEAR FROM YOUR HANDS WHAT YOU CAN."
— Ashanti Proverb

What are your thoughts on this quote?

Getting to the basics: It's a goals thing

If you want to make it somewhere you have to know where you want to go. Think about it, while you might discover something great if you just got in your car and went, you could still spend a huge amount of time just sitting in your car, or end up in old places because you didn't really think about where you wanted to go.

At the start of a therapeutic journey, I tell each new client that getting away from feeling horrible is great, but not the full picture. How will you know you have met a goal if you never actually set one? Sometimes we make lateral moves because we didn't take the time to think about where we are and truly consider where we would like to be. We can be so consumed by our excitement, fear, or impatience, that we make moves with no destination in mind, and go around in circles.

Think about where you would like to be at the end of this workbook. What would you like to feel? How would you like to interact with others? What do you want from the relationship you have with yourself, family, friends, and significant others? When we know what we want, put a date on it (like the one built into this book), we have a goal. When we know our goals, we are more likely to meet it, especially if we write it down. That's why we are doing a little goal planning.

Reminder: We will carry forward with moving in our truth. So be honest with yourself about what you want, no matter how small or grandiose.

What are you hoping to get from this workbook?

What are you hoping to address or confront within yourself?

What are you hoping to have the courage to discuss with friends?

What are you hoping to have the courage to discuss with family?

"IF YOU CLOSE YOUR EYES TO FACTS, YOU WILL LEARN THROUGH ACCIDENTS."
— *African Proverb*

What are your thoughts on this quote?

Pre-work WERK

Alright now! This is where we get to the basic facts, the things we already know to be true. We start this journey with a request that you be truthful. Why does it sound like I don't believe that you were going to start off with the truth? Because people lie. We lie to ourselves all the time for a multitude of reasons. We deny what we see right in front of our faces in favor of what we want to believe instead, or what we know to be the better answer in the eyes of others. We lie so that we don't expose our hurts to the world. But in this case, with this workbook, the truth is where we need to start. As raw and ugly as it might be, as hurtful and shame-filled as it may come, we need it. We need to expose our truths to examine them and begin the process of change. So, no, this is not the moment to "fake it till we make it." This is not the part where we practice positive thinking and deny what we truly feel. This is the time for you to be very raw and real, to stand in your truth. Let's not close our eyes to our facts and learn through unnecessary accidents.

Take a deep breath. Let's begin.

Getting to the Basics

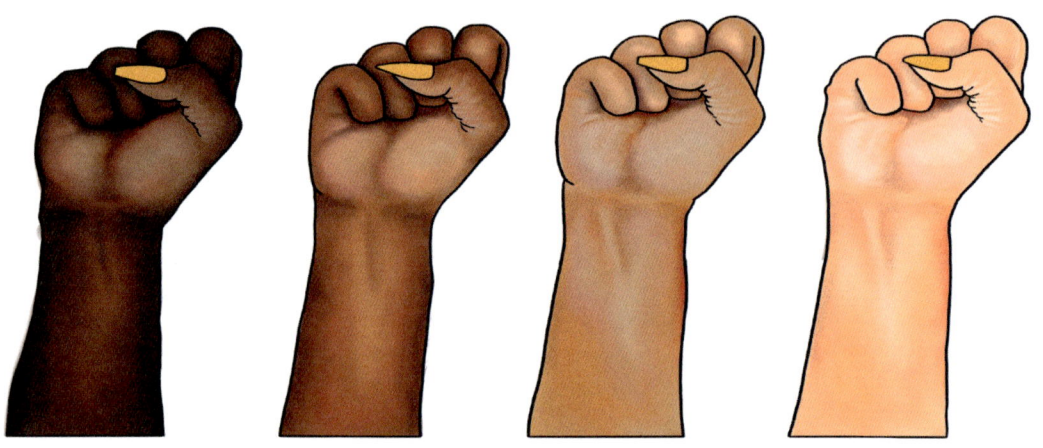

Getting to the basics: it's a skin thing
Getting to the basics is getting to the basic truths of you. Take some time to answer the following questions by filling in the blanks.

Using the picture, identify your skin tone. **Mark the shade that is most representative of your skin tone with a star.**

Using the same picture, identify the skin tone you would prefer to have. **Mark the shade that is most representative with the shade you would prefer with a triangle.**

What words would you use to describe your skin and skin tone?
Positive words

Negative words

Are you most likely to use the positive words, the negative words, or do you use all words at the same rate?

If you indicated that you would prefer a different skin tone, let's talk about why. First fill in the blanks, then **after** you have added your top 3 reasons for wanting a different skin tone, use the space below to talk more about your why.

(fill in the blank):
I usually notice that I would prefer a different skin tone when_____.

I seem to feel worse about my skin tone when_____.

The last time I noticed feeling this way was _____.

Things that seem to happen right before I feel some type of way about my skin tone are

_____.

My top 3 reasons for wanting a different skin tone are:

1.

2.

3.

Use the space below to talk about why you would want a different skin tone.

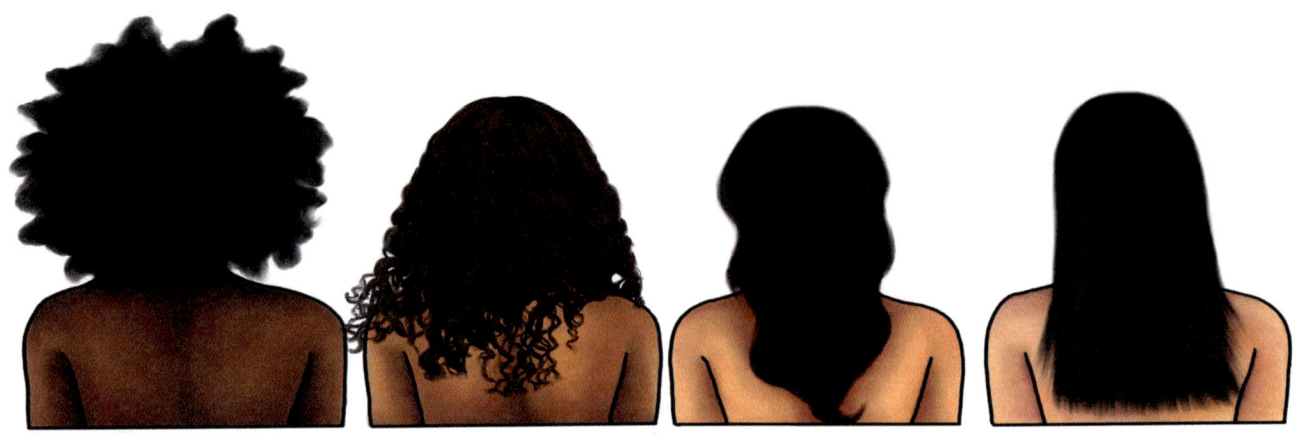

Getting to the basics: it's a hair thing

Using the picture, identify your hair texture. **Mark the hair texture that is most representative of your hair texture with a star.**

Using the same picture, identify the hair texture you would prefer to have. **Mark the texture that is most representative with the hair texture you would prefer with a triangle.**

What words would you use to describe your hair texture?
Positive words

Negative words

Are you most likely to use the positive words, the negative words, or do you use all words at the same rate?

If you indicated that you would prefer a different hair texture, talk about why. First fill in the blanks, then **after** you have added your top 3 reasons for wanting a different hair texture, use the space below to talk more about your why.

(fill in the blank):
I usually notice that I would prefer a different hair texture when _____.

I seem to feel worse about my hair texture when_____.

The last time I noticed feeling this way was_____.

Things that seem to happen right before I feel some type of way about my hair texture are

_____.

My top 3 reasons for wanting a different hair texture are:

1.

2.

3.

Use the space below to talk about why you would want a different hair texture.

"EARS THAT DO NOT LISTEN TO ADVICE, ACCOMPANY THE HEAD WHEN IT IS CHOPPED OFF."
— *African Proverb*

What are your thoughts on this quote?

Before I Let You Go....

Now that the PRE-Work Werk is done, I want to give you a few more reminders, notes, and pro-tips.

Reminders:
1. Pay attention to the things you may notice going on with you while doing the prompts or activities in this book. Write them down, reflect on them as much as possible. Try to let go of hurts while keeping the lessons you have learned.

2. You may notice that you feel some type of way while going through this. You can notice heightened feelings of anxiousness, sadness, irritability, etc. You may feel joy at some of the memories this will evoke, or you may feel sadness. Throughout, acknowledge what you are feeling (you can use a feelings chart to help). Give the feeling a name. Sometimes it helps to say it aloud. Deep belly breathing is also a great way of moving through it. I have included a link for you on guided meditation. When you feel like you need it, take some time (it's a 5 minute video) to listen and go through the exercise.

NOTE:
This is a process and will take time. However, through that process you can find that you feel different. That you see and feel and experience yourself and others around you differently. It can be scary to have all that change. Sometimes it may be necessary to pause and take it all in. Note what changes you are experiencing and what is good or bad or neutral about those changes.

But keep in mind there are always possible consequences, good and bad. On the good side: you may notice that you feel more confident. That you are loving on you in a whole new way of experiencing others differently. You may find yourself drawn to new things that you want to try. That's great! On the "bad" side: some of your relationships may change. Sometimes when we grow into loving ourselves on a new level, we realize that we may have been receiving love that isn't adequate for us. We notice that we may have accepted some things and folk into our lives that no longer fit with our vision. Now I have written about how to navigate changes, to communicate, and even let go as necessary, so if you find that is the case, you can find those blogs on Annodright.com/blog

Pro Tip: If you feel things really getting out of hand or pocket for you, seek help! Therapy For Black Girls is a great resource to start with.

One last thing, there will be tips and suggestions throughout the book. Try to consider some of the tips because like the quote says, listening to advice can help you in the long run. :)

Feelings Chart

Angry	Insecure	Cautious	Appreciative	Chill	Confused
Content	Dafaq!	Lovestruck	Disappointed	Unmotivated	Exhausted
Grieving	Anxious	Celebrated	Hurt	Impatient	Irritated
Overwhelmed	I Wish A B*itch Would **Aggressive**	Depressed	Unbothered	Optimistic	Frustrated
Relaxed	Guilty	Negative	Sad	Happy	Lonely
Ugh	Feelin' Myself **Sexy**	Envious	Withdrawn	Some Type of way **Undecided**	

Journal Prompts

This is where we really get to work! In this section you will find several writing prompts. Please, don't get intimidated and skip this section, this is the part you paid for! There are a total of 12 weekly prompts and two story time prompts. Each prompt is made for you to think about your answer in stages. Writing your initial thoughts, but then using the week to consider more and come back and write in the space journaling style.

While the idea here is to complete one prompt a week, giving you a glowing finish in about 3 months, you do not have to rush! If one prompt every 2 weeks feels better, then do that.

How can you complete the work, if writing isn't your thing? There are several ways to do this! Talk to text, is one of my favorite. Pull up your favorite program, say the question aloud, and say your answer. When you re-read to check for errors, chances are you will add to your answer. You can also just record your answers in a memo. Label the voice memo with the question, and you will be able to revisit it and consider your answer even more. You can also turn that audio into a written transcript so you can see your answer. Use a transcription service like Ollie or Rev to get this part done.

Pro tip: Doing this alone can feel intimidating. Get a few friends together who also purchased the book, and go through it together book club style!

"YOU MUST ATTEND TO YOUR BUSINESS WITH THE VENDOR IN THE MARKET, AND NOT TO THE NOISE OF THE MARKET."
— *Beninese Proverb*

What are your thoughts on this quote?

Week 1

#GettingBack Memories

Activity: Let's think of this activity as "memories from the corners of your mind." Take a moment to think back as far as you can. Think about what you were like back in first grade, or as far back as you can get. In each of the circle spaces below, I want you to take time to write out what you remember as being significant. I know this seems vague, but I want you to think about standout memories: good, bad, ugly, or indifferent. Some of these might be specific to hair texture and skin tone, but they don't have to be. They can be about partners, friendships, embarrassing or loving moments. It's about what stands out to you. Let's pick seven from the distant past—depending on your age, this could be elementary school, or even up to the end of college, seven from the recent past— we are talking about the last 3-5 years, and seven from the current sort of past—the last 6 months to a year. When you're done picking your 21 memories, let's put them on the timeline.

Distant Past

1.

2.

3.

4.

5.

6.

7.

Recent Past

1.
2.
3.
4.
5.
6.
7.

Current-ish Past

1.
2.
3.
4.
5.
6.
7.

Timeline

Place the distant, recent, and current past memories along the timeline in the order they happened. You will see we already started with your arrival into the world! Put your date of birth and go from there!

Birthdate:

Reflection Questions

What was it like to dig into your memory for this activity?

In looking at the memories you picked, were they mostly positive, negative, neutral, or a combo. Why do you think this was the combination?

What emotions and thoughts came up for you in doing this activity?

Week 2

Great! You have put your memories on the timeline and now it's time to get to the next part of this work. I have a few questions for you that I would like you to answer using some of the information that you put on your timeline. Here's the thing, this may get you thinking about some new memories that you would like to add to your popcorn list and then to your timeline. That's okay! Go ahead and add them. Here are your questions:

What made each of the memories you chose stand out?

Distant Past:

1.

2.

3.

4.

5.

6.

7.

Recent Past:

1.

2.

3.

4.

5.

6.

7.

Current-ish Past:

1.

2.

3.

4.

5.

6.

7.

How do these memories on your timeline play a role in your here and now?

How do each of the memories add to your narrative around your hair texture and skin tone?

Hair Texture	Skin Tone

How do these memories add to how you think of other folks hair texture and skin tone?

Hair Texture	Skin Tone

Week 3

If you remember way back in the pre-work WERK, you did a little form which eventually got you to picking out your top 3 reasons for wanting to change your hair texture and skin tone. This is where we carry on with that work.

Re-write the top 3 reasons you would want to change your
texture here:

1.
2.
3.

your skin tone here:

1.
2.
3.

Week 3 Alternative:
So you didn't feel the want or need to change your texture or your skin tone! Great! That means that your work is a little different. Since the other activity doesn't apply, let it fly. For you, I want you to think about the top 3 reasons/influences you have had that have helped you accept your hair texture and skin tone as they are. The folk who help us accept our hair may not be the same folk who support with skin tone love.
texture:

1.
2.
3.

skin tone:

1.
2.
3.

Now, using your feelings chart, what are the emotions that come up for you with each of these reasons? Keep in mind, some of them may overlap, but that's okay. List 1-3 emotions next to each reason.

Hair Texture

Skin Tone

Week 4

We are still building on the work we started last week. So, in the space below, write out those three emotions that can be triggered for skin tone and hair texture. After you have done that, I want you to think about the times when something happened and triggered the emotions you identified last week, What are some things you have done in the past to help make you feel better? List at least 5 of those automatic coping skills. Finally, talk about how each of those coping skills have been helpful or not so helpful in the moment and the consequences (good or bad) for that reflexive coping skill

emotions triggered:

1.
2.
3.

previously used coping methods:

1.
2.
3.
4.
5.

top 5 automatic coping skills: helpful   not helpful

1.
2.
3.
4.
5.

consequences of auto coping skills:

1.
2.
3.
4.
5.

"YOU HAVE LITTLE POWER OVER WHAT'S NOT YOURS."
— Zimbabwean Proverb

What are your thoughts on this quote?

Week 5

The build continues. Looking back at what your answers were for the coping skills and consequences, write down the skills that you identified as being effective and having good consequences. If you have less than 7, write in some coping skills you would like to try. Some examples of coping skills to try can include things like: journaling, painting, cleaning, cooking, or going to a walk/drive.

1.

2.

3.

4.

5.

6.

7.

Finally, on a separate sheet, write out your coping skills in an artistic way, decorate it, and place it somewhere as a reminder for what you can do when you are feeling particularly bad, sad, etc. about your hair texture or your skin tone.

Pro Tip: some of the coping skills you want to try might not work for you or won't work in every situation. That's why we have a whole list of them. When you recognize that something isn't working, add a new thing you would like to try instead. This way, your list continues to grow, and you can see just how many coping skills you've got on hand!

Creative Coping Skill Sheet

Week 6

#Message...?
Now that we have already started the memory jogging process, this prompt might not be too hard. If it is, take your time. You've got all week to consider this one.

What messages do you remember about hair (texture/length) and skin tone when you were growing up?

Consider and write: How did those messages apply or not apply to you?

For some of us, it was all too common to hear certain things said. Even if it wasn't said TO us, many times we heard it AROUND us. Sometimes we don't think about how we are impacted, for better or worse, by the things that happen around us.

The things we see, hear, and experience make an unforgettable mark which we can carry forward with how we think about ourselves, but also how we think about and interact with others.

Read the following common messages that folks have often heard or remember personally. Write down what you think and feel when you see them. Consider how they related or did not relate to you in your upbringing.

1. "You're pretty to be dark skinned"

Thoughts:

Feelings:

2. "She light skinned with that good hair"

Thoughts:

Feelings:

3. "She got pretty hair to be dark skinned, can you imagine if she was light?"

Thoughts:

Feelings:

4. "What are you mixed with?"

Thoughts:

Feelings:

5. "If you're white, you're alright. If you're brown stick around. If you're black get back, waaaayyyy back"

Thoughts:

Feelings:

6. "Her hair is nappy AF"

Thoughts:

Feelings:

7. "She think she all that because she is light skinned"

Thoughts:

Feelings:

How did they relate or not realte to your upbringing?

Story Time

It's STORY TIME!! But you will have to be the one to write it. Yeah, this is some BONUS work. This won't count for the weekly work, sorry, not sorry. This is separated out because I want you to record your Hairstery and/or Skin story. Think of this as a very specific autobiography, focused on talking about the history of your hair and skin tone. You have done some real work by now that you can draw from with digging up memories, recording them, and answering some (arguably) tough questions. But you haven't been able to write the story in its entirety and see how how all things come together. So this is your chance!

Use the questions/prompts below to help you write out your Hairstery and Skin Story. Your story can be intertwined with skin tone, or you can write it out separately.

> **Pro tip:** it might be easier to write it out as two different stories first and then bring them together, so nothing gets lost:

1. Write out your HAIRSTERY (the history of how your hair texture showed up in your life): Relate it back to the significant moments that you've put on your timeline, add new ones as you think of them. Remember to think about not only hair texture, but also hair length.
    - Examples of some things to put in your story: Did you ever wear a towel or t-shirt on your head? What was it like to get your hair done?
2. Write out your Skin Story (the history of how skin tone showed up in your life): Remember to think about your skin tone, but also if your skin was clear, oily, smooth, dry, etc. Those things also play a role in the memory
3. Think and write about how your hairstery and your skin story intersect. **
    - Did any of the things you remembered from your hairstery and skin story show up on your timeline?
    - Now that you are thinking about your hair texture history, and your skin tone history, how have they played a role in some of the good, bad, ugly, and in different memories from your timeline?
    - What about where you skin story and the hairstery intersect, how did the intersection show up on your timeline? How do those moments and memories match up or not match up to some of what you have on your timeline?

** right about now, someone is probably wondering why am I asking you about how your hair texture and skin tone stories intersect. I asked because when we talk about hair texture, we also talk about skin tone and vice versa. There is the idea the one can save you from the other, if one is not ideal. For example, having lighter skin can "save" you from the "shame" of kinky hair textures and having that "good" hair texture can save you from too dark skin tones.

So when we explore one, we inadvertently talk about the other, or conflate the two. Think about this: Tatyana Ali from the *Fresh Prince of Bel-Air* showed up in the documentary *Light Girls*, though arguably, she is not light skinned. She does, however, have a naturally straighter hair texture. So, how have the two (hair texture and skin tone) intersected in your life interactions from the past? Here are two questions to consider in answering this question:

1. What do you remember learning about beauty growing up?
2. What do you remember learning (good or bad) about yourself and how you looked from family members? Friends? People in school?

Your Hairstery:

Your Skin Story:

Intersecting hair and skin:

Great job doing that extra work! Now back to our regularly scheduled programming!

"THERE CAN BE NO PEACE WITHOUT UNDERSTANDING."
– African Proverb

What are your thoughts on this quote?

Week 7

This week we are talking about values! Values are the things that a person thinks of as being most important. Values can determine what is prioritized and help you make choices based on those beliefs.

The thing is we often learn our values from family first, since they are usually our first encounter. But we learn values from way more places than just home with the family. We learn values from our friends, from tv and movies, and we learn values from school. Each person we meet can have something different that they value above all others, which offers us a different perspective. All of our life experiences also help us determine our own values, and what we ultimately take in and stick with.

BUT sometimes we don't live according to the values we have been taught or the ones we adopt for ourselves. When we don't, we can feel some type of way, maybe dissatisfied or even restless. When we do live according to our values, we can feel a whole lot better. But often times, we don't think about where our values have come from OR whose values we (might still) follow. The questions this week are designed to help you think about the values conveyed to you either through folks' words or their actions as it relates to your hair texture and skin tone.

VALUE LIST: here is a list of common values. Please note this is NOT exhaustive, so feel free to add your own if you feel something is missing for you!

Love	Wealth	Family	Morals	Honesty	Humor
Loyalty	Reason	Success	Knowledge	Power	Friends
Free time	Adventure	Independence	Achievement	Beauty	Spirituality
Fun	Calmness	Freedom	Recognition	Nature	Popularity
Responsibility	Peace	Respect	Variety	Stability	Wisdom
Fairness	Equity	Creativity	Relaxation	Safety	Modesty
Ambition	Logic	Pride	Justice	Diversity	Humility
Courage	Cunning	Sisterhood/Brotherhood			

What values do you think were presented to you regarding what you looked like from Family? Friends? Peers? Others?

What values did you have back in the day (when you were younger) about your hair texture and skin tone?

What values do you have now around hair texture and skin tone?

How have those values changed over time?

Whose opinions and values have mattered the most where it came to your looks when you were growing up? Make a list. You can include actual people and their names, or categories of people. Make sure to include yourself on that list. Put them in the order from the most important to the least important.

1.

2.

3.

4.

5.

Now, make a value list for current times. Whose values and opinions take up the most space currently? Make your list of the top 5 from the most important to the least important.

1.
2.
3.
4.
5.

Things to consider: Did you make your top 5? If so, where did you land on your list? What about your list (if anything) do you want to see changed? What values do you want to have?

Week 8

There are many components that make us who we are. But, for many, those concepts are not always self-identified. People judge us daily on what we wear, how we present, the way we speak, the job we have or don't have, if we are in a relationship or single, how much money we appear to make, how tall, short, thin, fat, pretty, ugly, light and/or dark we are. Judgements are constantly and consistently being made. Assumptions about who we must be and how we live our lives. While those things may not be or truly define WHO we are, they can impact our identity.

Sometimes we play up what others think about us. Sometimes we fight against it. There is the middle road, of course, where you are simply unbothered. However, that is very rarely the case. We have been bred to be bothered. Even to say you aren't is to show others that you are still impacted.

So for this week, take some time to think about how hair texture and skin tone may have impacted your identity. Think about how your identity with family, friends, at school and/or work, in romantic relationships, when traveling, and when you are home alone. Make sure to think about positive impacts **and** negative impacts.

Romantic Relationships:

Positive Impact:	Negative Impact:

Reflection:

Work/ School:

Positive Impact:	Negative Impact:

Reflection:

Family:

Positive Impact:	Negative Impact:

Reflection:

Friends:

Positive Impact:	Negative Impact:

Reflection:

How does your hair texture play a role in your identity? If it doesn't play a role, how do you know and why doesn't it?

How does you skin tone play a role in your identity? If it doesn't play a role, how do you know and why doesn't it?

How does your hair texture and skin tone impact the way others identify with you in various settings (think home, school, work, etc.)

One thing I know is that sometimes, our very friendships can be put to the test based on hair texture and skin tone politics. We choose our friends for a multitude of reasons, but sometimes it could be based on how they look and how we feel in comparison to that. Maybe it confirms your cuteness or maybe it makes you feel like you are in competition. Regardless, we can feel friendships getting strained because we have a difference of opinion about the impact skin tone and hair texture can have when you go out. The point is, I have seen more than a few clients who talk about how they are navigating friendships with folk who don't understand what it's like to be in their skin tone or have their hair texture. So this exercise it meant for you to look a little bit more into how hair texture and skin tone politics might come up within your friendship(s).

Name 3 to 5 of your closest friends.

What do they look like in terms of skin tones and hair textures?

How do you feel when you are in their presence? Just hanging out alone? In public together?

How have values and messages informed these feelings?

Have you ever felt like you were in competition with them or they with you based on how you look? What did that look like?

MONTH 3

"THE FOOD THAT IS IN THE MOUTH IS NOT YET IN THE BELLY."
—Kikuyu Proverb

What are your thoughts on this quote?

Week 9

Remember that timeline you created back in week one? I know it's been awhile. Flip back and take another look. This week marks more than 2 months worth of work! You are already toward the end of this journey! To cap it off, I wanted to help you make more of an illustration about how one thing flows into the next.

We have been spending a lot of time in the past. We have looked at what happened, the messages we got, and how they impacted us. we have looked at values and even taken some time to think about who we are with special consideration given to the hair on our heads and the skin tones that adorn our bodies. But how do we bring this home? How do we use this work to press forward? We look at it again!

What we have learned in various areas of our lives, both explicit lessons and implied learning, takes root and flows forward. When I think about it, I almost see a stream. White supremacy tells people of color that they are worth less, and that if you are Black, you are at the bottom of desirability. Patriarchy, and the sexism it upholds, tells us that if you are a woman or femme that you are not as valuable as men or those with male/masculine bodies. That intersection can be especially harrowing for women of color, considered to be worth less by race and less valued by sex. These messages are taught in various ways. They are taught with who we see and don't see in movies and tv shows. By which characters get to be the protagonist in books and in storylines and who gets shunted to be the best friend. By who gets paid what and how voices are valued or ignored at the proverbial "table." We learn "our place." But we don't necessarily think about the way one message flows into the other and impacts us and how we live our lives.

Here is a flow that I often see:

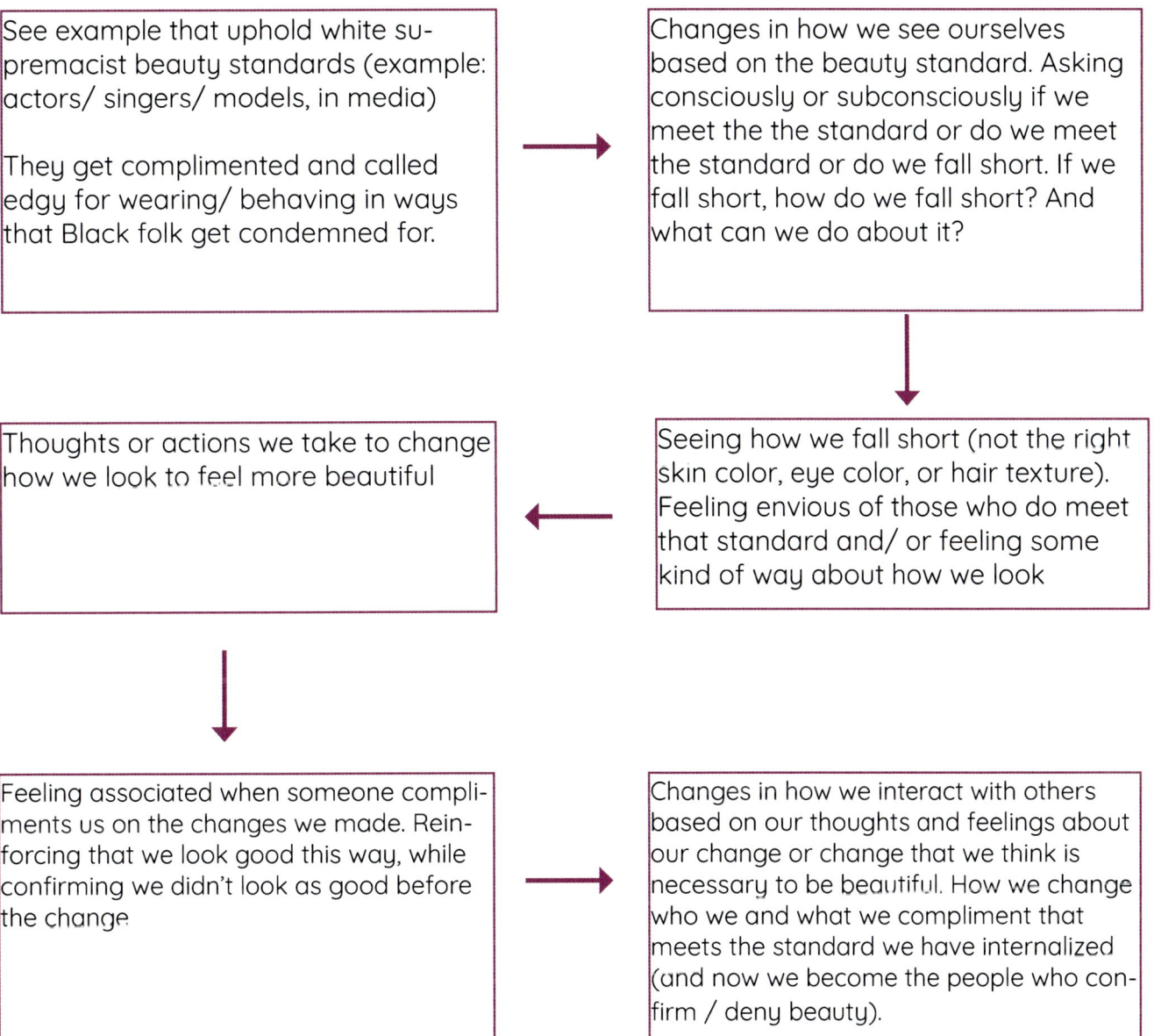

This can seem complicated, but it's not. It is more about how one thing flows to the other! When I was doing my research on hair texture and people were talking about WHY they returned to natural hair, one thing that kept coming was that they didn't want to inadvertently give the message to their daughters that they had to change what they look like to be considered pretty or valuable. That's one hell of a flow!

Fill in Image:

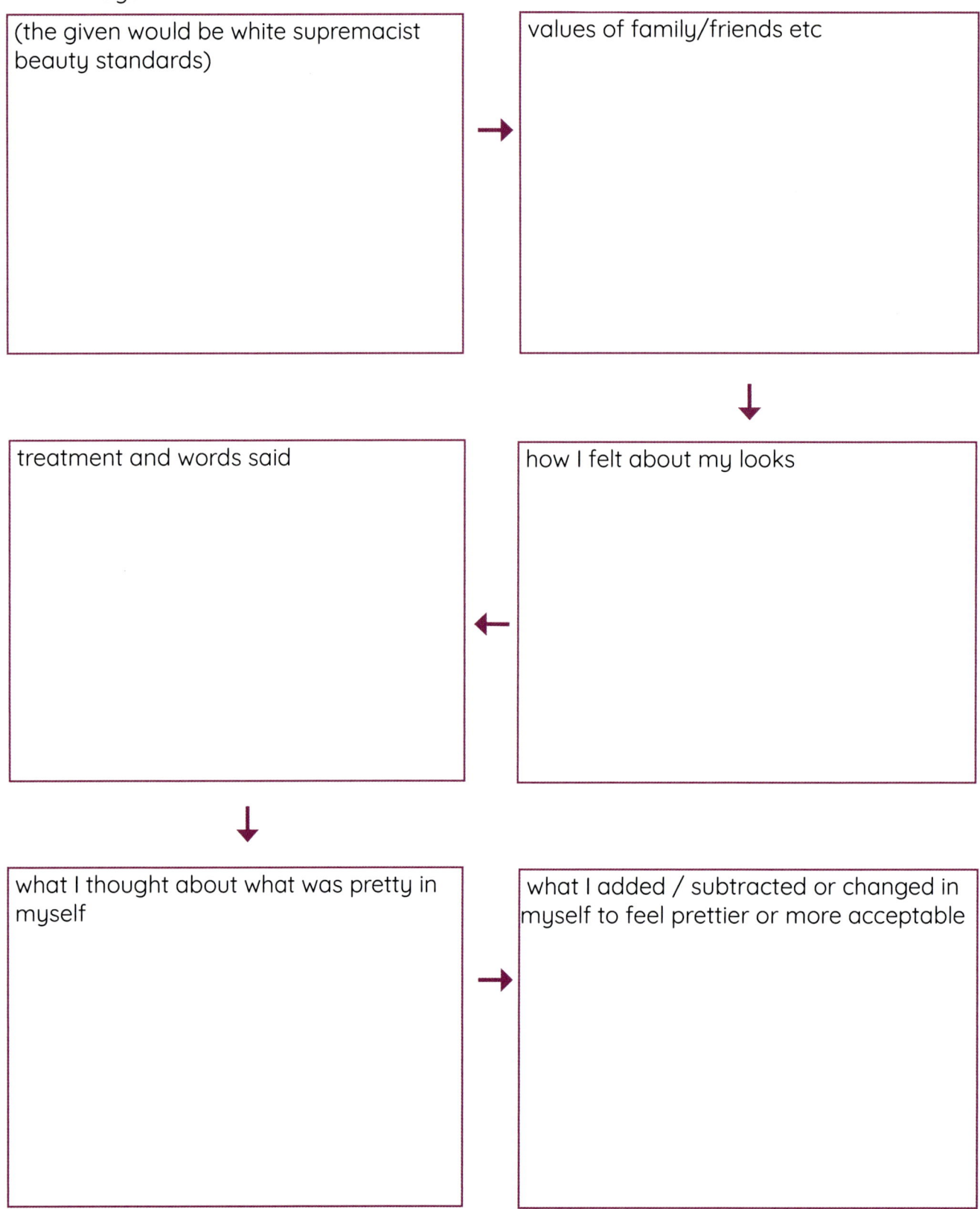

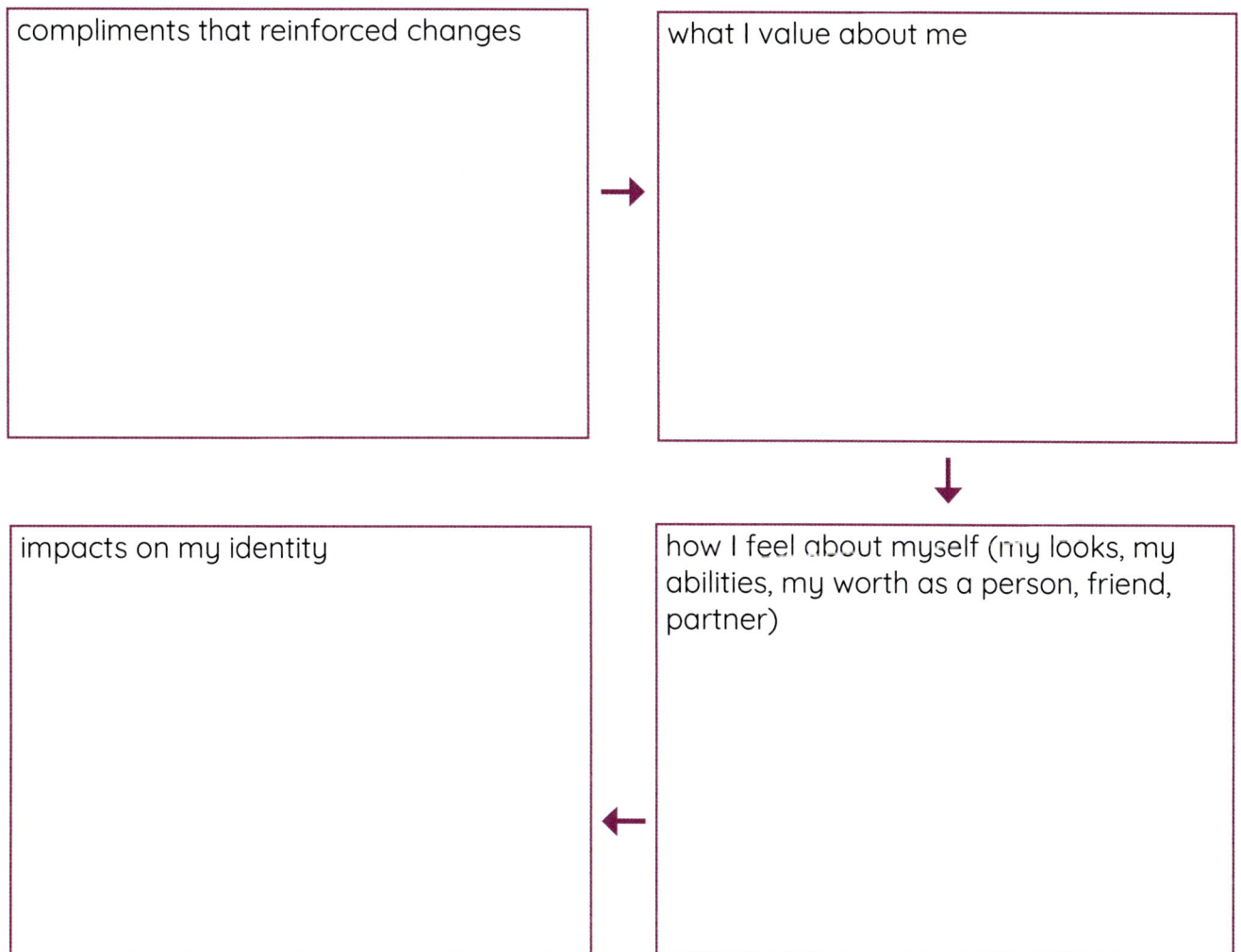

Why did I have you do this activity? I wanted to make sure that you understand that even if you grew up with some hurtful messages around skin tone and hair texture, those messages are heirlooms passed down. It becomes our intergenerational baggage. This baggage, filled with hurts, slights, and messages of the day, often go unexamined, though they can still be (potentially) harmful. It is up to us to unpack the baggage and to learn to travel a bit more lightly.

Week 9 Reflection:

Week 10

Now, I know you have to have noticed that when you are somewhere you've been before versus somewhere you have never been that your comfort level changes. It happens for everyone! With me, for example, when I was working for an agency in the DC area, I was super comfortable with my fellow co-workers for the most part. But, things always seemed to shift when upper management was there, and shifted even more if a lawyer or a guest was present. You start to watch what you are doing, be more careful with your words. Some people even shift the way they, sit, stand, or how they talk.

Have you ever noticed how your comfort level changes with your hair in certain spaces? How about your skin tone? Have you ever noticed your hair or skin tone impacting any area of your life? Which area? (ex. Some folk feel more confident if they straighten their hair for an interview. Or feel a little less confident when dating if they don't have a certain look).

What flaws do you think you have? How have you tried to change those flaws? How have you tried to accept them?

What day is it? It is Challenge Day!

> "IF YOU WANT TO GO FAST, GO ALONE. IF YOU WANT TO GO FAR, GO TOGETHER."
> *—African Proverb*

If I remember correctly, I told you this workbook would have activities and challenges. Well, hopefully you have already seen that there is a whole section for activities and a section for challenges. But this is NOT a challenge you will find listed there. But nevertheless, this here is your first challenge!!! How exciting?!?!?!!

What's the challenge: 14 days of praise. For 14 days you will compliment your hair and/or skin tone on one thing. It can be as small as complimenting that you have hair or as big as ...anything you want!

Who is doing it: YOU are! If you tag me on IG, Twitter, or FB @Annodright, I will see if we can recruit a crew and do it together! I'd love to help hold you accountable.

In the space below, write in what you are praising your skin and hair for. At the end of the day, come back, and write out how it felt and what impact it had on you (and dare I say, others?)!

1. Praise:

Impact:

2. Praise:

Impact:

3. Praise:

Impact:

4. Praise:

Impact:

5. Praise:

Impact:

6. Praise:

Impact:

7. Praise:

Impact:

8. Praise:

Impact:

9. Praise:

Impact:

10. Praise:

Impact:

11. Praise:

Impact:

12. Praise:

Impact:

13. Praise:

Impact:

14. Praise:

Impact:

WOW! You have hit 14 days! Looking back on it, what did you notice? Did it get harder or easier as the days went on? Did you notice any changes about your inner voice? What did you notice about how you interacted with others?

Week 11

Opinions are like buttholes: We all have them! Let's examine some of yours.

When you hear/see the words 'texture envy' or "texturism" what do you think of?

How do you think texture envy relates to the idea of good/bad hair dynamics?

When and How does texture envy manifest in your life? (how does it come to you? How do you give it to others?)

How do your values play a role in this thought process?

How does your identity play a role?

Week 12

Ahhh! The last week! Back in week 6, we gathered some of the hurtful messages we may have received or heard as a child. Today I want you to tear out that page and on this page, write some new messages that you would have liked to hear instead about your hair and skin tone. Things that uplift you and make you feel valued, loved, and beautiful.

AFTER you have written out new messages, take each negative message you received, ball it up and tell that person (figuratively) that this message no longer applies to you. Then throw that message away! Say your replacement message out loud after you ball up each of the negative messages you received. This is our way of symbolically throwing away the old, and embracing the new.

> "WE DESIRE TO BEQUEATH TWO THINGS TO OUR CHILDREN; THE FIRST ONE IS ROOTS, THE OTHER ONE IS WINGS."
> —*Sudanese Proverb*

What are your thoughts on this quote?

Not Another Story??!!?

Of course there would be! I asked you to write about your past hair and skin life a few weeks ago. AND you have spent a great deal thinking about who you are right now, haven't you? It seems only fair that after having done all that work, that you get the chance to create your own future.

What would you like your HairStery of 5-10 years in the future to say and reflect?
What do you want to think about your hair texture?
What do you want to think about your skin tone?
How is that conveyed to others around you?
What is the legacy around your hair texture and skin tone that you want folk to be able to see, recognize, and remember about you?

Pro Tip: use some of the new and improved messages from the week 12 prompt.

"SMOOTH SEAS DO NOT MAKE SKILLFUL SAILORS."
—African Proverb

What are your thoughts on this quote?

Activities

You've found the activity section! What follows includes coloring pages, word searches, and crossword puzzles. This is a space for you to take a break but still think about skin tone and hair texture. Because while smooth seas don't make skillful sailors, we can't always over do it with rough seas either. We need balance and a break.

Hair Grease Crossword

Down:
1. Caused by damage to the hair's cortex
2. Portmanteau for the date you went natural
3. Racist terminology for softer, looser-curled hair; also, a 2009 documentary directed by Chris Rock
5. Used to keep hair moist and detangled
8. Term used to describe the part of hair at the nape of the neck that was entirely resistant to hair-straightening methods.
9. Hair intertwined closely to the scalp using braiding techniques that may involve three or more sections of hair
13. Rounded natural hairstyle, gained cultural prominence in the 1960s and 70s

Across:
4. Extensions woven or glued into the hair via tracks
6. _____ knot, a hairstyle featuring small, coiled buns throughout the hair
7. Creator of the Hair Typing System
10. Chemical-based mild form of relaxer
11. A length of plain or patterned cotton cloth wound around the head
12. Term for unrelaxed, unpermed Black hair

Cocoa Butter Crossword

Across:
6. Colloquial term for a light skinned black woman
8. Track #12 on To Pimp a Butterfly
13. Patches of skin darker in color than the normal surrounding skin
14. Treating people differently based on the social meanings attached to skin color
15. Patches of white skin
16. Cultural movement originating in the 1960s to promote Black beauty
17. Small brown spots on the skin
18. Term to describe person who prefers lighter skin over dark skin

Down:
1. Term for skin in need of moisturizing
2. Adage denoting melanin's ability to protect against signs of aging
3. Used to gain acceptance in the the early 1900s to upper class Black societies
4. A dark brown pigment occurring in the skin
5. Song played over the opening credits of Get Out
7. Sweet made from roasted and ground cacao seeds
9. Preferential treatment based on lighter pigmentation - "light skin _____"
10. Balm that makes blemishes and scars fade
11. Nobel prize winning author of The Bluest Eye
12. The second single from India.Arie's debut album

Hair Grease Word Search

```
L S E S S E R T G T E X T U R I Z E R L E R X
I I C O R N R O W S N A P P Y E G A K A E R B
F R B A N T U K N O T S G G E S R A O C S T D
L E H H A I R T Y P I N G S Y S T E M G C E I
U L G B L A R U T A N M A E T E A Y N E O N A
F A H O U B J R P H C U O T T N O D V U L D L
F X E B K R K H Y Y V G H O T C O M B S H E D
Y E A B I A E V L H E S L A O G R I A H A R E
M R D Y N I G Y R J Y V E S A E R G R I A H H
C B W P K D A G U T W I S T O U T U G P Q E C
M O R I Y S K Y C Y V N E E R U T X E T M A T
J N A N Y M N Y R E K L A W W E R D N A C D A
Q N P S L X I Y E P E D G E S V K W E A V E N
R E A M I A R D E S S E R P B U N D L E S D S
X T I W O B H V S O F T R E N O I T I D N O C
A G A W C T S H C M A D A M C J W A L K E R H
```

Find the following words in the puzzle. Words are hidden ↑ ↓ → ← and ↘.

- DON'T TOUCH
- BANTU KNOTS
- SHRINKAGE
- BONNET
- FLUFFY
- HEADWRAP
- RELAXER
- COARSE
- COILY
- TENDERHEADED
- CORNROWS
- CURLY
- HAIR GOALS
- EDGES
- BRAIDS
- BOBBY PINS
- HAIRGREASE
- HAIR TYPING SYSTEM
- TWISTOUT
- PRESSED
- KINKY
- LAID
- LOCS
- MADAM CJ WALKER
- NAPPY
- BUNDLES
- BREAKAGE
- TEXTURIZER
- HOT COMB
- TEXTURE ENVY
- ANDREW WALKER
- TEAM NATURAL
- TEXTURIZER
- TRESSES
- SNATCHED
- WEAVE

Cocoa Butter Word Search

```
B B C A Y N O B E F O B S I D I A N N F D J B
U N H A N E D L O G W O L L E Y H G I H A A B
T R O R U B C A R A M E L Y E Z N O R B R L D
T S C L U F I T U A E B S I K C A L B N K L E
E A O Q T M M E L A N I N F R L Y E N O H I S
R B L F M A S B N I P P O P N I N A L E M N S
P D A B C I N N A M O N R E B M A F S G G A I
E N T C I E C O M P L E X I O N M G Z D N V K
C O E O Z N G O Q R A G U S N W O R B F V H N
A M F C H S O R P F Y E L L O W B O N E I C U
N L P O X U E N O B D E R F M U I D E M B N S
B A G A B H D T H G I R B T H G I L A Y R E A
R S M O O T H J T H G I N D I M C O P P E R H
O W Z I C O F F E E M A H O G A N Y U A X F C
W A X C O L O R S T R U C K D R L G C W I J O
N X Q T D D M D R E T S A B A L A L I G H T M
```

Find the following words in the puzzle. Words are hidden ↑ ↓ → ← and ↘.

CHOCOLATE
ALBINO
ALMOND
AMBER
BLACKISBEAUTIFUL
BRONZE
BROWNSUGAR
BUTTER PECAN
BROWN

CARAMEL
ALABASTER
CINNAMON
COCOA
COFFEE
LIGHTBRIGHT
COMPLEXION
COPPER

DARK
EBONY
MELANIN
POPPIN
GOLDEN
HIGHYELLOW
HONEY
LIGHT
COLORSTRUCK

MAHOGANY
MEDIUM
CARAMEL
FRENCHVANILLA
MIDNIGHT
MOCHA
OBSIDIAN
REDBONE

SMOOTH
SUNKISSED
TAN
YELLOWBONE

87

Collecting Compliments

This activity right here requires you to not only reach back in to the memories, but also to stay present as you move forward. Keep a running log of the compliments you receive that make you feel great!

Why do this? Because, we often have trouble truly accepting compliments and will deflect instead. So this one is to encourage you to accept compliments and let them hit home.

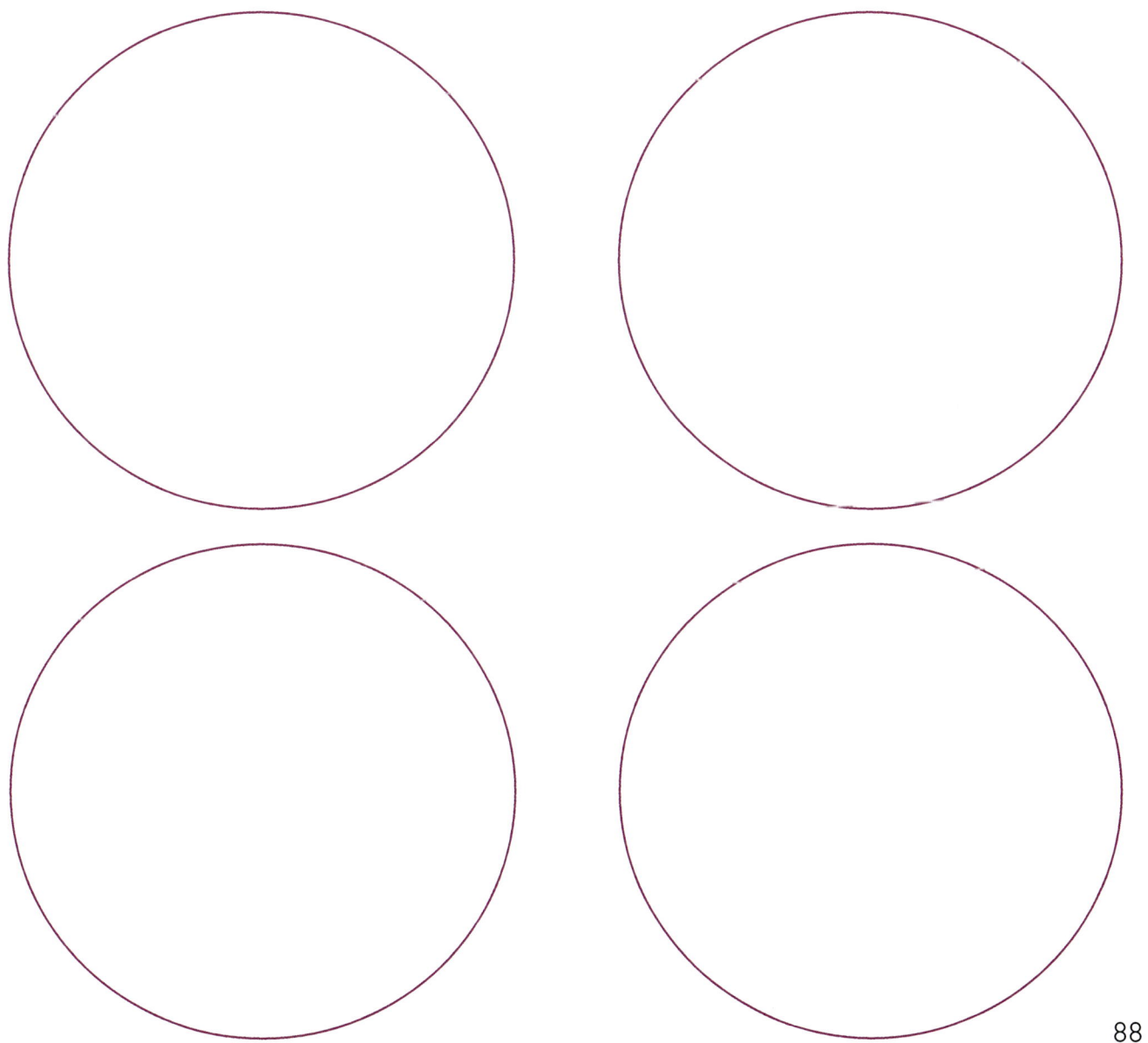

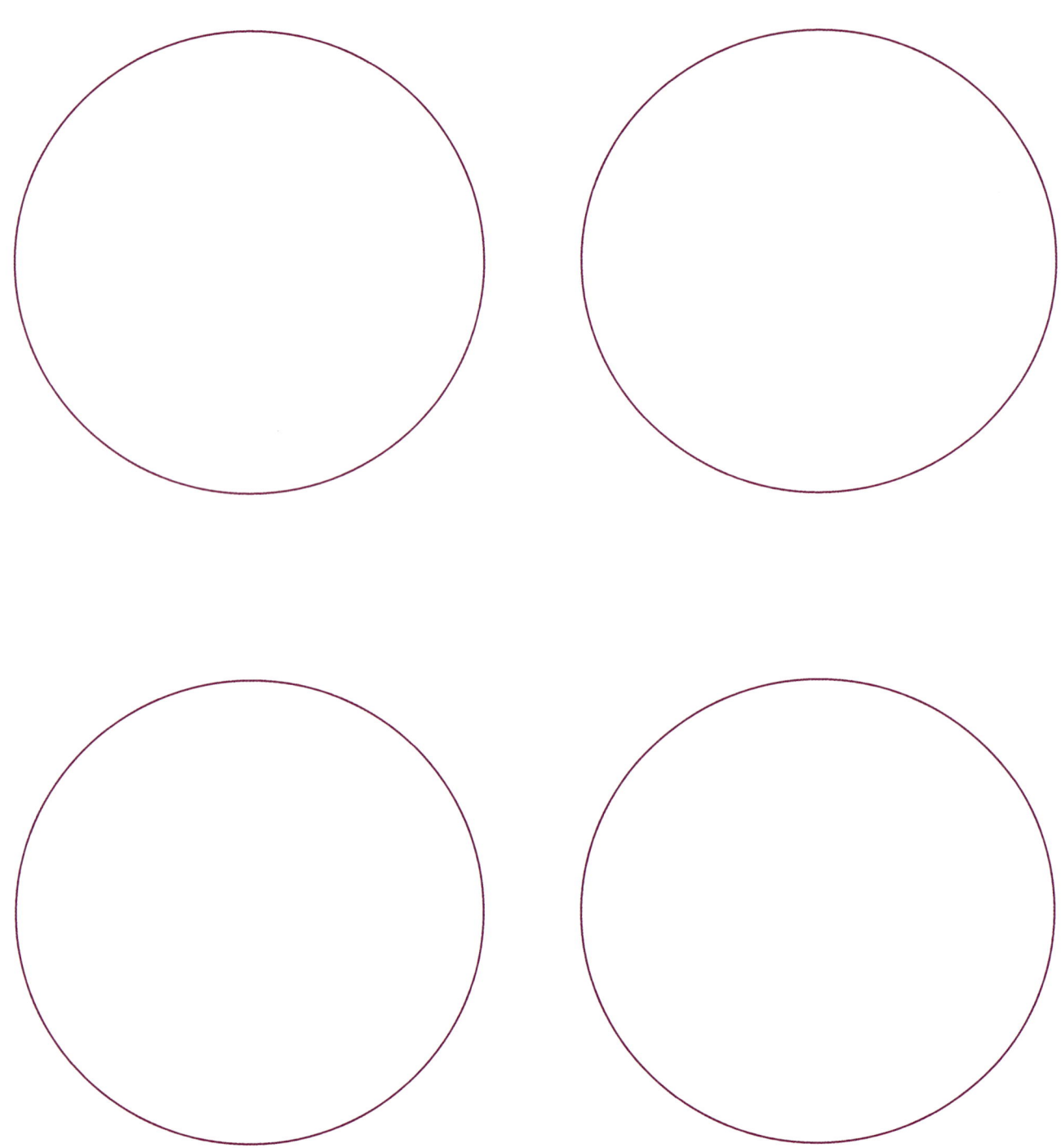

How Do You See You, Boo?

For this activity, the goal is to see you in triplicate. What you'll need: color pencils or crayons.

Directions: Take a moment to think about how others see you. What do they think of your hair? How do they react to your skin tone, etc? Now, in space #1 make a visual representation of that. Next, think about how you see you. What do you think about your hair and skin tone? How do they make you feel? In space #2: Draw a visual representation of how you see yourself. Finally, think about how you WANT to be seen. In space #3 Draw a visual representation of how you would like to be seen. DON'T FORGET: to label your pictures. You want to be able to understand what you meant later :)

Box #1

Box #2

Box #3

Reflection: What did you notice was different from the three pictures you drew?

It's Coloring Time

"SUGARCANE IS SWEETEST AT ITS JOINT."
—African Proverb

What are your thoughts on this quote?

Challenge Day Continues!

You are doing all the mental/emotional work and I appreciate that! Here is some more practical work for you to try your hand at! Please note, that anything you see here, has not only been tried by me, it is work others have done at some point or another!

The purpose of these challenges is so that you can learn more about your hair texture. Often folks get discouraged on their hair journey because they feel their hair is not manageable or can't create the looks they saw on someones IG or Youtube. But that notion is usually based in trying to achieve something that may not be yours to achieve. Meaning that styles achieved most easily for those with naturally straight hair are going to need different techniques and will take a different effort for someone with the kinkiest coiliest hair. Trying to get hairstyles that only straight long hair can get is futile when you have a teeny weeny afro and only leads to disappointment, discouragement, and feeling some type of way about your hair. So to help you learn and love the hair you actually have, we have some challenges and assignments!

P.S. yes, this part focuses more on hair, but that doesn't mean you should stop looking. There are also challenges in here for skin tone. Some of them are the same or similar challenges.

For some of these challenges, you could feel some type of way, like I am coming for you or judging you. I promise I am NOT coming for you because of WHAT you do to your hair. The focus here is on the WHY. What are those reasons behind the reasons we give ourselves and others about how we fashion/sculpt ourselves to be in public. Example: sometimes we tell ourselves that certain styles are simply more professional. But while you may straighten your hair, that's not the focus. The focus is on WHY you straighten it. On why you feel straighter hair is more professional.

This is space for you to challenge those notions that say you can only show up IF you show up how others want or expect. That you can only show up if you show out in ways that are often seen as being acceptable. Why do you wear a wig or gel your edges? What are the origins for the practice, when did you subscribe to them, and why do you keep up with them? Don't get me wrong, wigs, braids, and weaves aren't inherently bad, but when we use these things, along with being natural, (yes, some folk use being natural as a cover up, too) to cover up pieces of ourselves from shame, lack of acceptance, etc. ultimately, we are the ones who lose out on ALL the pieces of ourselves. We lose ourselves. And we lose our sense of direction and purpose. We lose our self acceptance and love. We become lost. Beasts in a forest of our own making .

Now is where we find ourselves and remember that WE are the bag, and WE need to secure ourselves. Whether we feel like we are jangling freely with our 5 pieces in a small change purse or a whole stack that requires duffle bags, suitcases, and a bank. I want you to cash in on ALL of you. So here we go!

Whatcha Lookin' At?

Nothing gets you thinking something is wrong with you faster than constantly seeing the same images that don't reflect your beauty! So, let's add some diversity to what you are seeing in the feed so you can know your beauty is reflected in others!

Pro tip: In this challenge you can choose to focus on hair texture or skin tone.

- Find a natural hair enthusiast whose hair texture and length are SIMILAR to yours! That means leaving those other Youtubers with hair down to their knees, alone. Find 3 video makers or IG folk who have hair texture similar to yours and follow them. Make sure to take in something they do at least 1x/week.
    - BONUS: if you are already doing this, AWESOME! But your challenge will be to find 3 more to follow to grace your IG, FB, or Twitter feeds.
- For those using this challenge on skin tones. Find some folk with lush hues that seem close to yours. Make sure to follow those who have a message you want to see, but also spread it out so that it's not all just smooth brown skin. Pimples, discoloration, etc. are things of beauty too. They all map the life of your face and body

3 Natural Hair Enthusiast:

3 Lush Toned Folk:

How hard were they to find?

What do you hope to learn/get from them?

What was it like when you first started following them?

after 1 month of following:

after 2 months of following:

after 3 months of following:

And Not an Edge was Laid!

Yup, the title tells all. Lay no edges for the next two weeks. Why? When we get into our beauty routines and practices, we can sometimes tie our worth to them. That we are only worthy of respect and attention IF we do certain things. The same thing can go for edges. Do you always have to have them laid to the gods when you step out of the house? Or are you able to go busy edges and all to run your errands and know some folk might still try to talk to you? Just Askin'.

How long will you go without laying the edges?

How did you feel on day one?

How do you feel now that you are done with the challenge?

What was it like to go out without laying your edges?

What is something you learned about yourself?

Seek and Ye Shall Find

Find and try to execute one new hairstyle a month. It helps to remove you from a rut on how you style your hair. AND helps you to learn what your hair might be willing to try with you.

Pro tip: Try this one at a time when you can be patient with yourself. If it turns out bad, who cares. If it's great, go out with it and show awf!

Pre styling:
What is the hairstyle you want to execute?

When will you try it out?

Post Styling:
What was it like to try out the style?

What did you learn about your hair?

How did you feel after everything was said and done?

Need a hand?

What's that one thing you've always wanted to do with your hair but were too scared to try? For me, I have NEVER dyed my hair. I really wanna see what my 'fro would look like if it were blue!

What makes you scared of doing it?

Do you think you would be brave enough to try it now temporarily? Find your pro and make it happen! Please note: I am NOT telling you to try a perm for the first time if that is not your jam. Why? Because it's kind of permanent! BUT if you have ever wanted to wear a full on Beyonce weave, or wear a cute short style, now is your time to try!

Reminder: I said find a pro! Don't get mad at me if your friend messes this all the way up. Get someone with skills that you trust or don't come for me! When you've done it, take before and after pics and tag me on IG, Twitter, or Facebook @Annodright, so I can see how flyy you look! (psst: I'll post when I have my blue hair!)

No Braid Zone!

Sometimes we use braids as a way to cover up our hair hurts related to texture and/or length. And while we rock those beautiful braids we can create more distance and resentment with our own tresses. So, let's take a break! I've personally done this at multiple times in my life for different lengths of time. The shortest was 3 months, the longest was a year. I learned a lot about myself and my tresses in that time. So, pick your increment, and just say NO! Just wear and love your hair the way it is.

Pro tip: this is a great time to try out a new style sans braids

How long will you go without getting braids: _____

What have you been learning about yourself and your hair?

What was it like to do with challenge?

Were their temptations? How did you manage them?

Wash and Wear!

I know lots of folk feel like they already do this. Das cute! What I mean is learn your hair as it is. So, no, we aren't stretching our hair or manipulating the texture with twist outs.

What is your actual unaltered hair texture?

What does it feel like when it's wet? Dry?

When you put creams in it?

How can you style it?

How can you manage it?

Reflection:
What was it like to go as a true wash and wear without stretching? What did you learn about your hair?

Slow Down!

Our skin is our largest organ. And while we may put lotion on and rush our butts out the door, sometimes we don't appreciate it. So now we slow down. Take a luxurious bath or steamy shower. Touch every inch of your skin and note how it feels to do so. When putting on your lotion, take your time. Massage it into your skin. Notice the smoothness, roughness, etc. Notice where your skin is sensitive. Notice how your skin looks and feels when you are done.

What do you appreciate about your skin?

What did you notice?

What was it like to slow things down?

Pay for Nothing

This is one of my favorite challenges. I did this one for a year. The goal is not to pay for any services for your hair except for clipping your ends and maybe a protein treatment. Other than that, if you want that braided style, or that new twist out, you have to find a friend or family member to help you out. This is to help you build community and positivity around your hair with others. No cheating!

Pro Tip: Trade off with who does your hair. By doing their hair in return, you keep things equitable AND can learn some skills that can help you with your own hair.

Who are your FREE community hairdressers?

What was it like to connect with people around your hair?

"When the food is cooked there is no need to wait before eating it."

Kikuyu Proverb

What are your thoughts on this quote?

You have done it ALL and then some! From pre-work werk to weekly journals. From story time writing to challenges. How do you feel now that you have finished the book?

You made some goals when you started, now we examine what you feel you actually got. Did you meet the goals you set at the beginning? If so, what's next? If not, what other steps can you take to meet it?

What did you get from this workbook? How does what you got from the workbook compare to what you were hoping to get?

What did you address or confront within yourself? How does what you were hoping to address and confront compare with what you were able to confront? Is there more work you would like to do with this? What is that work?

What do you have the courage to discuss with friends? Is there anything missing from what you were wanting to have the courage to discuss? What conversations will you have? With Who? When?

What do you have the courage to discuss with family? Is there anything missing from what you were wanting the courage to discuss?

Did anything shock or surprise you in your answers or thought processes in going through this workbook?

Hopefully at this point in your journey, you have learned a lot about the narratives you have received about your hair texture and skin tone. Hopefully you are feeling more aware and empowered to craft the life you want to live with special attention to your hair and skin.

Please note that the journey doesn't stop here. There are levels to this. Unraveling the messages can take a lot of time and consideration. When we think we made it, we realize there is a new level. That's okay. Write down what comes to mind, and keep this work going! The question is:

How are you going to continue this work?

What are the goals you have for the super future and what steps can you take to be more conscious of the relationship you have with your hair texture and skin tone, and ultimately you?

Hair Grease Crossword Solution

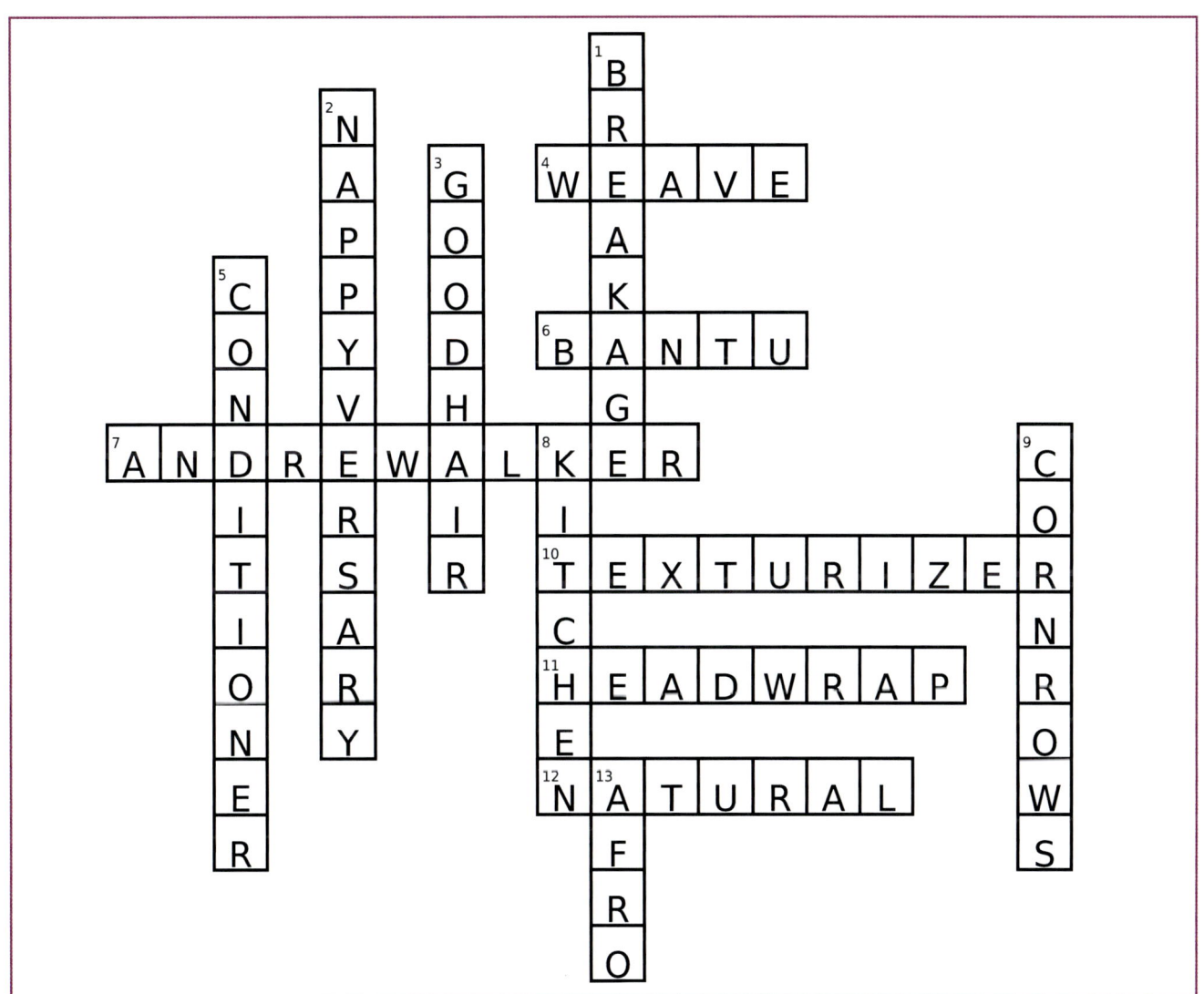

Cocoa Butter Crossword Solution

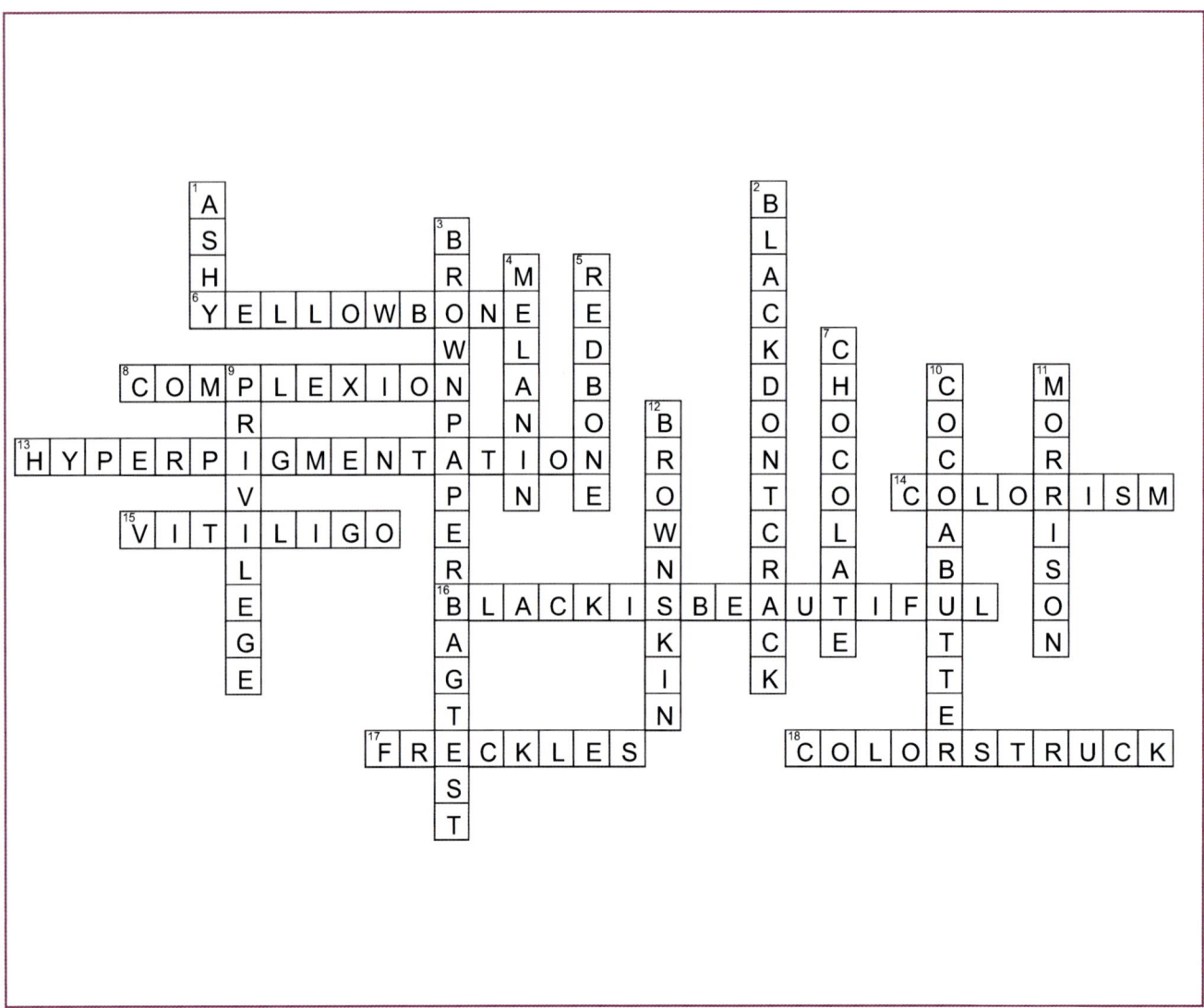

Hair Grease Word Search Solution

```
. S E S S E R T . T E X T U R I Z E R . . . .
. . C O R N R O W S N A P P Y E G A K A E R B
F R B A N T U K N O T S . . E S R A O C S T D
L E . H A I R T Y P I N G S Y S T E M . C E I
U L . B L A R U T A N M A E T . . . . . O N A
F A H O . B . . . H C U O T T N O D . . L D L
F X E B K R . . Y . . . H O T C O M B . . E D
Y E A B I A E . L . . S L A O G R I A H . R E
. R D Y N I G . R . . . E S A E R G R I A H H
. B W P K D A . U T W I S T O U T . . . . E C
. O R I Y S K . C Y V N E E R U T X E T . A T
. N A N Y . N . R E K L A W W E R D N A . D A
. N P S L . I . . . E D G E S . . W E A V E N
. E . . I . R D E S S E R P B U N D L E S D S
. T . . O . H . . . . . R E N O I T I D N O C
. . . . . C . S . . M A D A M C J W A L K E R .
```

Cocoa Butter Word Search Solution

```
B . C . Y N O B E . O B S I D I A N . . D . .
U . H . N E D L O G W O L L E Y H G I H A A .
T . O . . C A R A M E L . E Z N O R B R L D
T . C L U F I T U A E B S I K C A L B . K L E
E A O . T . M E L A N I N . . . Y E N O H I S
R . L . A . . N I P P O P N I N A L E M N S
P D A B C I N N A M O N R E B M A . . . . A I
E N T C I . C O M P L E X I O N . . . . . V K
C O E O . N . . . R A G U S N W O R B . . H N
A M . C . . O . . . Y E L L O W B O N E . C U
N L . O . . E N O B D E R . M U I D E M . N S
B A . A . . . T H G I R B T H G I L . . . E A
R S M O O T H . T H G I N D I M C O P P E R H
O . . . C O F F E E M A H O G A N Y . . . F C
W . . C O L O R S T R U C K . . . . . . . O
N . . . . . . . R E T S A B A L A L I G H T M
```

Resources

Therapy For Black Girls: www.Therapyforblackgirls.com
- This is a great resource if you are looking for a Black woman therapist in your area. The directory is national, so you should be about to find someone with relative ease.

5 Minute meditation: annodright.com/blog/2018/guidedrelaxation
- Use this video if you feel yourself getting a little anxious. It's 5 minutes and guides you through to getting to a (hopefully) calmer state. Don't worry, it's free :)

Deep Belly Breathing:
- This one is for when you are on the go. Deep belly breathing is also great for calming down when you are getting to be a little anxious. Go to the link to learn how to deep belly breathe. Because believe it or not, yeah we may be breathing people, but it doesn't mean we know how to breath to calm ourselves.

An Open Path:
- This is another resource if you are looking for a therapist, but you don't have insurance and can't afford the rate of some of the folk in the TFBG directory. There is a one time sign up fee, but therapy session from a therapist found on this directory will cost between $30-60 per session.

Feelings Chart
- Especially created for this workbook. You will find it on page 23. Please use this as a way to identify the emotions you may be experiencing. But note: the list is in no way exhaustive.

Pro tip & reminder: you may be feeling more than one emotion. Try picking the top 3 and writing about those.

Things I like that talk about hair and/or skin:

Movies/TV
1. Spike Lee's *School Daze*
2. *Dark Girls*
3. The "*Black Like Us*" episode of Black-ish
4. *Good Hair*

Music:
1. "Brown Skin" by India Arie
2. "Don't Touch My Hair" by Solange
3. "No Lye" by Shelly Nichole Blakbushe
4. "Afro Puff" by Lady of Rage
5. "4 women" by Nina Simone

Books:
1. Hair Story by Ayana Byrd and Lori Tharps
2. The Politics of Black Women's Hair by Althea Prince
3. Hair Matters: : Beauty Power and Black Women's Consciousness by Ingrid Banks
4. Hair Raising: : Beauty Culture and African American Women by Noliwe M. Rooks

Instagram Folk:
1. Rachel Elizabeth Cargle @rachel.cargle
2. Dr. Yaba Blay @fiyawata
3. Kheris Rogers @kherispoppin
4. Buelah Davina @thecreamycrackrehab
5. ME! Dr. Donna Oriowo @annodright AND @cocoabutter_hairgrease

YouTube:
1. Grapevine TV, season 3 episode 14 "Natural Hair"
2. Naptural85, you can also follow her on IG

Pro tip: You can find more things I like, with links, including my favorite hair and skin care brands on COCOABUTTERANDHAIRGREASE.COM! Go there now and hit the "notify me" button to stay in the loop!

Add the things you like that talk about hair and skin.

1.
2.
3.
4.
5.
6.
7.
8.
9.
10.

Meet the author

Dr. Donna Oriowo (Oreo-Whoa!) is an international speaker, clinically licensed social worker, sex & relationship educator and therapist, oh, and now, an author! Located in the Washington D.C. metro area. Dr. Oriowo is a first-born, first- gen Nigerian-American, book reading, school loving, therapy doing, passionate teaching, founder of AnnodRight! AnnodRight's mission is to bring intersection of sex, sexuality, culture, race, hair texture, skin tone, etc. into not only the therapy office, but all of her work. Dr. Donna is dedicated to helping others reclaim their sexuality, identity, and self love with an emphasis on addressing mental health, intersectionality, culture, and race in both educational and therapeutic settings. This is important because to her, Black Sexuality Matters, especially Black Female Sexuality. Dr. Donna has completed keynotes, presentations, trainings, and workshops that fill the gap and assist Black women and couples in finding their sexual freedom, while being culturally relevant.

The Doc collects inspiring quotes, travels to expand her mind and shift her worldview, gives firm handshakes, warm hugs, and knocks on the head. Dr. Oriowo currently serves as part of the Diversity, Equity, Inclusion committee with AASECT and is a member of Women of Color Sexual Health Network (WOCSHN). She can be found on Facebook, Instagram, and Twitter @Annodright. OR you can visit her (day or night) at www.AnnodRight.com or www.donnaoriowo.com.

References

1. Bellinger, W. (2007). Why African American women try to obtain 'good hair'. Sociological Viewpoints, 23, 63-72.

2. Byrd, A., & Tharps, L. (2014). Hair story: Untangling the roots of black hair in America (2nd ed.). New York: St. Martin Press

3. Hunter, M. L. (2002). "If you're light you're alright": Light skin color as social capital for women of color. Gender and Society, 16 (2), 175-193. Stable URL: http://www.jstor.org/stable/3081860

4. Newman, B. M., & Newman, P. R. (2009). Development across the lifespan: A psychosocial approach. Belmont, California: Wadsworth Cengage Learning

5. Oriowo, D. O. (2016). Is it easier for her? Afro-textured hair and its effects on black female sexuality: A mixed methods approach (order No. 10120151). Available from Dissertations & Theses @ Widener University; ProQuest Dissertations & Theses A&I. (1805610606). Retrieved from http://0-search.proquest.com.libcat.widener.edu/docview/1805610606?accountid=29103

6. Pearlman, M. (2018, October 23). The origin of the term 'intersectionality'. *Columbia Journalism Review*. Retrieved from: https://www.cjr.org

Made in the USA
Monee, IL
26 January 2020